Rosa Young
Hero of Faith

By Christine S. Weerts

Illustrated by Larry Johnson

CONCORDIA PUBLISHING HOUSE • SAINT LOUIS

Copyright © 2011 Concordia Publishing House
3558 S. Jefferson Ave., St. Louis, MO 63118-3968
1-800-325-3040 • www.cph.org

Written by Christine S. Weerts
Illustrated by Larry Johnson
Edited by Rodney L. Rathmann
Editorial assistant: Amanda G. Lansche

Manufactured in Burlington, WI / 034280 / 160012

Table of Contents

Rosa Young

Rosa stopped and looked out at the sea of white.

◆ ◆ ◆

chapter one

Into the Cotton Fields

Rosa ran out to her family's cotton fields, just past their home deep in the woods of rural Alabama. It was 1897, and everyone she knew grew cotton. On this warm November day, she was proud to help with her first cotton harvest. She hurried because she didn't want her older brothers to get too far ahead.

At the edge of the field, the seven-year-old stopped and looked out at the sea of white. Just days ago, it had been an ordinary field of knee-high green plants. Suddenly, with enough sun and dry weather, the cotton bolls had popped open, turning it into a field of white. It reminded her of that verse her Daddy liked to preach: "Lift up your eyes, and look on the fields; for they are white already to harvest" (John 4:35b KJV).

A mighty will made up for Rosa's small size. When her father tried to give her a child-size sack to fill, she said quietly but firmly: "I'm no baby, Daddy."

"All right, Rosa Jinsey Young, here's your Big Girl bag," he said, smiling.

Rosa crisscrossed the big burlap bag over her tiny shoulders. She wondered how she would ever fill it. But she had begged her father to let her come—he had wanted her to wait a year before working in the fields—so she wasn't about to complain.

She had watched her brothers pick cotton whenever she had brought them water. She was sure she knew what to do: you pull the white fluffy cotton boll out of the pod. Here, her small size was an advantage: she didn't have to bend over the plants like her father and brothers.

But she also didn't have their rock-hard calloused fingers. Whenever she reached into the rough brown shell to pull out the cotton boll, one of the ragged edges scratched her finger. She bit her lip to keep from crying out, but no matter how carefully she picked, she couldn't keep the pods from slicing her fingertips.

As the autumn sun rose higher, the bag got heavier and heavier. Her fingers were throbbing with dozens of tiny cuts. Pushing back the tears, she kept picking, even though her brothers were so far ahead she couldn't see them. Her breath grew short as she tugged the heavy bag and wiped the sweat from her face, smearing the black dirt from the fields across her forehead. She was tired, but she would not give up.

She decided to distract herself with her favorite daydream: she's standing in front of a group of little children and teaching them to read. Rosa had never been to school, but she had the dream that someday she could teach her people to read, like her daddy was teaching her.

"Rosa, Rosa," her father called to her. Rosa had passed out in the field. She came to as her father picked her up, along with her half-filled bag of cotton. To her it had seemed so heavy, but he lifted it like it was filled with feathers.

Before she could protest, her father hushed her. "You did fine for a first try. Let's go get you some water and some rest."

On the way back to the house, Rosa reached across her father's back to give him a hug. She felt a strange bump. It was long, snaking all the way across his back. She reached down farther, there was another one. "Daddy?" she said, knowing somehow that he was not going to answer.

"You did fine for a first try. Let's go get you some water and rest."

Alone in the house with her mother and her sleeping baby sister, Rosa worked up the courage to ask, "Mama, what are those long bumps on Daddy's back? They feel ugly."

The house was still. Even the chickens clucking and scratching in the dirt yard seemed to hush. Rosa saw tears fall from her mother's eyes. Had she said something wrong?

"They are from a time that was ugly, child. From days we don't ever want to go back to."

Rosa saw tears fall from her mother's eyes.

Rosa's mother told her about her father's childhood and her own—both had been slaves. "I was not much older than you are now when Mr. Lincoln freed us."

"It was bad times," she continued. "You only counted as someone's property. You were scared that at any time, you could be sold away from your family on the auction block."

"They sold our people?" Rosa asked, choking on a sob.

"Yes, darling. And split up families. Lots of our people never saw their children or parents again. Masters could be that cruel.

"Your daddy worked for a wicked man like that. Mr. Clem was known far and wide for his mean streak. One day, he got mighty mad. He took your father out to an old oak tree, tied him to it, and grabbed a cat-o-nine tails. Your father's mother once told me she could still hear the screams of that whip cutting through the air and slicing open your daddy's back.

"That devil man musta whipped your daddy 10 times—that's how many of those bumpy scars run all across his back. Ol' man Clem finally quit.

I guess he was afraid he might kill your daddy—
and then he'd lose his property. Your daddy, he was
only 14, but he was strong. He slowly walked back
to his shack and collapsed while his mama rubbed
ointment on his wounds."

"Why did that mean man whip Daddy?"

"No telling. White man don't need no reason.
We were their property. They could do as they pleased.
He could whip for working too slow, trying to run
away, breaking an old rake, talking back, even for
reading a book!"

Whipped for reading? How could that be? Rosa wondered. Learning about the world through books didn't hurt anyone.

"Back then, it was illegal for slaves to learn to read and write, Rosa," her mother said.

Rosa's heart nearly burst as she thought about not being able to read! She cherished her one book, that old blue-backed speller. When it disappeared last week she looked for it everywhere, panicking. How happy she was when she finally she found it stuck in the wood plank wall.

"Mama, I'm going to be a teacher. I want my people to read!"

Rosa began thinking about those old kindly folks she visited with her mother, who took them plates of corn bread, ham, and greens. There was the old couple, the Ramseys, who once shared a slice of melon with little Rosa, even though they didn't have enough for themselves. Dear Uncle Simon, who was loved by white and black alike for his fair-mindedness and good sense, and sweet Aunt Penny, who was crippled, and always asked her to read a chapter of the Bible that laid on her lap.

"Were they slaves, Mother?" she asked.

"I'm afraid so," her mother said. "There weren't but a handful of free black in our backwoods area. The rest of us were owned by white folks—some of them are neighbors today. Your granddaddy even has the name of his owner, Mr. Bonner."

Rosa felt tears on her cheeks. It hurt her to think about her people in slavery and not being allowed to read. She thought about the children living around her right now who had no schools to go to.

Finally ready to share her cherished secret, she said, "Mama, I'm going be a teacher. I want my people to read!"

Rosa taught her younger brothers and sisters.

chapter two

Give Me Jesus

"Sheffield Lorenz Young!" twelve-year-old Rosa sternly called her younger brother's name. "Pay attention. I told you to memorize your numbers. Now, repeat after me: $5 \times 2 = 10$, $6 \times 4 = 24$, 7×9 is-"

"Sister, I cain't. You're mixing 'em up. Besides, I'm tired," Sheffield said, stifling a yawn. "I been in the fields all day."

Rosa was tired too. She had worked in the field before daybreak, then walked two miles to the old church where she took classes. She returned at dusk to finish her chores, help with cooking, and now teach her younger brothers and sisters before doing her own schoolwork.

"Why do I hafta larn all this mess for anyhow? No one else do," he said.

Sheffield was right. None of the children in their backwoods community knew how to read, write, or do figures. It broke Rosa's heart to see another generation of her people growing up illiterate.

But how were they supposed to learn?

Because of segregation, the state's meager education dollars were supporting two school systems, one for whites and one for blacks. And the white schools got most of the money, the better teacher salaries, new books, real school buildings, and even desks.

There were few schools for black children; most classes were held in old run-down churches. Often, there were no chairs, much less desks. The books were old and had to be shared. Sometimes the only way to stay warm was to make a fire in the churchyard.

And most schools only held classes two to three months a year—between cotton crops.

Just one generation out of slavery, many black teachers had little schooling themselves. Rosa remembered her first class when she was eight. When the teacher found out that she already knew how to read and recite the alphabet, she sent her home.

Her uncle, a student at Tuskegee Institute, had taught her the few times he was home, but mostly she taught herself with her spelling book and her cherished Bible. Two years ago, she had been baptized at her father's African Methodist Church.

Sometimes the only way to stay warm was to make a fire in the churchyard.

*Mostly she taught herself with
her spelling book and her cherished Bible.*

Now she was taking regular classes with a
trained teacher, but she would finish sixth grade in
another year. There were no public high schools for
blacks in her county.

She thought of her neighbors. Unlike her
parents, who owned their own land, most farmed
on shares, rarely making enough each year to pay
the interest on what they had borrowed to farm
that spring. Children didn't have enough to eat; it
brought tears to her eyes to see their misshapen,

malnourished bodies. They wore rags and went barefoot year round. Most families lived in old homemade shacks put together with whatever wood they could find, a chimney made of homemade bricks and a sheet of tin slapped on the roof. No wonder they boiled in the summer and froze in the winter.

How could her people ever climb out of such deep poverty without an education? she thought.

Her head was spinning, until she heard her brother: "Sister, what's wrong?"

"Sheffield, God has given you a good mind," she said, back in her firm role as teacher. "You got good parents who raise you right."

"Now, I expect you to learn these lessons. Our people have a lot of catching up to do," she told him. "You have to help lead the way."

Rosa, too, wanted to lead the way, but then she got sick. Her mother knew something was terribly wrong when Rosa did not get up for school. Cold, rain, bare feet, nothing kept Rosa away from school.

When a doctor finally came, he called it "rheumatism," and said the pain would come and go over the years. He was sure Rosa would never walk again.

But he didn't count on the prayerful determination of his patient! After eight weeks, Rosa forced herself to get up and hobble around with a cane. After a year using crutches, she was walking again. Though plagued with sickness throughout her life, Rosa pushed ahead. When she finished her sixth-grade education, she was back in the fields.

Give me Jesus, give me Jesus, you can have all this world. Rosa sang one of her favorite songs while picking cotton. She loved the "plantation songs," with their haunting melodies and simple yet soulful messages: Give me Jesus, Jesus only.

She knew these songs, called Spirituals, were first sung by slaves—like her parents—working in the cotton fields. *Give me Jesus,* Rosa kept singing, thinking of the mighty faith of her people. Slaves turned those terrible times into soul-filled haunting music that filled her heart with deep joy.

*"Rosa, your people should educate you,"
said Mr. Harper.*

She looked up and saw someone riding up
on a big red saddle horse. It was the landowner,
Mr. Harper. Today she was helping her family by
earning cash working Mr. Harper's fields.

"Rosa," he said, "You like school don't you?"

"Yes, sir, Captain," she said, using the name
all her people called him.

"You teach the children their books at night don't you?"

"Yes, sir."

"Rosa, your people should educate you."

As he rode off, Rosa thought of how hard she'd been praying to go to high school, promising God she would serve Him. Could this be an answer to her prayer?

In the small community of Rosebud, it didn't take long for word to get around that one of the white community leaders had said Rosa should get an education. Grant and Nancy Young began talking about where to send their daughter to school. They finally chose a private African Methodist church school in Selma, Payne University. With her money from picking cotton, Rosa could just pay for her train fare, clothes, and books.

◆ ◆ ◆
chapter three
Rosa Gets an Education

When Rosa and her father arrived in Selma that fall evening in 1903, bright streetlights shone next to tall brick buildings lined up along a paved street. For a country girl used to the dark sky in the deep piney woods, dirt roads, and small two-room wood shacks, she felt like she'd been caught up in the air and put down in another world.

The next morning that new world stretched in front of her: She walked down paved sidewalks, clicking her shoes against the unfamiliar cement. She touched the painted houses, in hues of greens and yellows. She ran her hands over the grass yards. It was so different from the unpainted log huts, dirt yards, and rough woods she was used to.

Her joy at her "new life" was short lived. As soon as she walked onto campus, she stood out from everyone else. City kids had never seen a country girl before: much less one that showed up two months late because she was . . . picking cotton!

"Did you see that new girl? She's so . . . country."

"Yes, look at those awful clothes," said another. "Looks like she made them herself. And what about those clunky shoes. Guess she wore those in the fields!"

"I can't get over her hair. Do you think she ever put a straightening iron to it?"

As soon as she walked onto campus, she stood out from everyone else.

Every time Rosa opened her mouth to speak, girls giggled at her "backwoods accent."

Adding to her embarrassment, she had to walk to the freight yard every week to pick up her food. Her parents sent her cabbages, corn, and greens they had raised. There was no money for "fancy" city food.

Just 13, Rosa wanted to run away. But she didn't have a dime to her name. She was a stranger in a foreign land.

"Please give me the strength to hold on," Rosa prayed.

"Lord," she cried out one day, "You got me here. I want to learn. Please help me," she cried. Study, cry, and pray, every night and every day— that was all she could do. Even when she scored high on the placement test, she was still resented.

Finally, after several weeks of ridicule, Rosa slowly began to make friends. But too soon it was time to leave for home—two months before the school year ended—to work in the cotton fields. She studied every chance she could, and her cotton wages again paid her way back to school, where she again arrived two months late.

As her classes became more demanding, Rosa had to work long hours catching up with old lessons she had missed and keeping up with the lessons she was taking. She rarely got to bed before 1:00 a.m.

A mean-spirited landlady made her life even more miserable, demanding that she wash her bedding daily, scrub the floor, and cook breakfast before school. She stole Rosa's food, so Rosa went to bed hungry, and took her kerosene, so Rosa shivered while doing her lessons.

"Lord, you answered my prayers and helped me get here," she prayed. "Please give me the strength to hold on."

Despite her shortened school years, Rosa's star was shining. From country laughingstock she soared to school favorite. She served as editor of the school newspaper, won first place in speech and math contests, and, finally, in her last year, was elected senior class president. An essay she wrote, "The Value of the Bible," was so popular it was printed and sold throughout the city to raise funds for the school.

Finally, the big day came: graduation, June 1, 1909. All her prayer, perseverance, and hard work had earned her the top spot as class valedictorian! She chose "He who is greatest is a servant," based on Matthew 23:11, as her theme—though she was so nervous, she delivered her speech sitting down.

"Let us not hesitate to do something worthy for mankind," she told her classmates. "Give light to those who are in darkness, sustain the weak and faltering, befriend and aid the poor and needy.

"Let us not hesitate to do something worthy for mankind."

"Our people need our best efforts, our bravest words, our noblest deeds, our tenderest love, and our most helpful sympathy," she said.

Within weeks of graduating, Rosa passed her state exam and received her teaching certificate to begin her service to her people and to her Lord.

Many rural schools for black children were empty because there weren't enough teachers. A discriminatory law stated that a public school that failed to meet during a school year had to return its state funds, which would be given to the white schools.

Wanting to keep schools for her people open, Rosa decided to teach in as many vacant schools as she could each year. She began her life's work at a little Baptist church in Piny Woods called Coonslide. Four months later, she taught at Pine Grove Church in Autauga County.

Always the sole teacher, Rosa had from 45 to 100 children in her classes. As time went on, she taught black children in even more remote communities across the state.

She prayed daily for the children in her care.

     She prayed daily for the children in her care.
One day at recess, watching the half-clad children
playing baseball with a rock and sticks in the dirt
yard, she began dreaming a bigger dream: her own
school. It would be a real schoolhouse with books,
not a rundown church that let the rain inside and
old borrowed books that were falling apart.

Education for the head, hand, and heart, she thought. She would teach the Bible, not superstition, and she would offer students the best education, not second-rate learning. And she wanted to offer a full school year, not just two or three months between cotton crops.

She had been teaching two years when she got a letter asking her to return to Rosebud to teach. "This is where I'll start my school, in my own home community," she prayed.

chapter four

An Answer to Prayer

A little bug, less than a half inch in size. How could something so small bring such hard times? How could a beetle destroy a dream?

The boll weevil arrived in Alabama in 1914, just two years after Rosa had single-handedly raised the funds to build and equip a new school for over 200 children in her home community of Rosebud, AL.

The weevil chomped its way into central Alabama from Mexico, feeding on the developing plant and destroying field after field of cotton, the largest cash-producing crop in the state.

The weevil chomped its way into central Alabama from Mexico, destroying field after field of cotton.

Rosa looked on the poverty of her people and felt a painful longing in her soul. Slavery was a terrible sin, and its consequences were still felt throughout her backwoods community, where her people who had come from nothing were still scratching out a living on land they didn't own.

Many black farmers, who worked shares or were tenants, had nothing to harvest and still owed the landowner for seeds, fertilizer, and other costs. The failed cotton crops sunk a poor state into deeper poverty and forced many blacks off the farm, starting the Great Migration to industrial cities in the North. For those left behind, despairing poverty and hunger were common. What would happen to the children if she gave up now?

At her school, attendance dropped as families had no money to help pay the costs. By the end of the school year in 1915, she had 35 cents left for her own salary.

She recalled the first lesson she had taught her students.

Every day she prayed: "God take my school, do not let it die but make of it a great religious center."

The strong tie to the children was forged over those long months and muddy miles, where she traveled by foot or mule, to make her dream come true. With her life savings of $200, and gifts from black and white friends, she had built Rosebud Literary and Industrial School, which opened in 1912.

She recalled the first lesson she had taught her students: **Life + Christ = Success**.

"There may not be a cotton crop," she said to herself. "But surely there is still a harvest to be made among my people. My life plus Christ can bring success!"

Rosa offered her school first to her home church, African Methodist, but their conference was unable to take it. After several other rejections, she wrote the one man in Alabama who cared about education for their people as much as she did: Booker T. Washington, founder and president of Tuskegee Institute.

"Try the Lutherans," wrote Booker T. Washington.

Surely this great educator and leader of her people, who himself had come up from slavery, could help her!

Dr. Washington wrote back saying he had no resources, but told her to contact a church she had never heard of, saying it was providing an education for white and black people. "Try the Lutherans," he wrote, giving her the address of Rev. C. F. Drewes in St. Louis.

October 27, 1915

Dear Friend,

I am writing you concerning a school I have organized. I began teaching here in 1912 with seven pupils in an old hall where the cattle went for shelter. I have bought with money collected in the community five acres of land and erected a four-room school house, bought 45 seats, five heaters, one school bell, one sewing machine, one piano, a nice collection of useful books, and 150 Bibles and New Testaments.

I am writing to see if you will take our school . . . we will give you the land, the school building and all its contents. . . . The school is located near the center of Wilcox County, 54 miles from Selma amid nearly 1,500 colored people. Both white and colored are interested in this school. I hope you will see your way clear to help us.

Yours Humbly,

Rosa J. Young

The letter was like no other Pastor Drewes had ever received. "I am sure I'm hearing the Gospel call, like Paul heard from Macedonia," he later wrote (referring to Acts 16:9–10). Immediately, he sent his faithful missionary Rev. Nils J. Bakke to Alabama.

On a cold night in December 1915, Rev. Bakke arrived by train at the station in Neenah, near Rosebud. He carried both a crutch and walking stick, and he even wore three different coats against the

On a cold night in December 1915, Rev. Bakke arrived.

chill of the night as he stepped off the train. This Norwegian Lutheran pastor, crippled and in his sixties, seemed an unlikely powerhouse for bringing the pure sweet Gospel to the Black Belt of Alabama.

But the journey to lead Rosa's people "out of darkness into light" is exactly what this preacher of the Gospel began.

With a heart for the people, Rev. Baake taught at the school and led the forming of a congregation. Many ex-slaves and older children who attended church could not read, so Rev. Bakke tirelessly taught then to recite the Lord's Prayer and the Apostles' Creed.

Every Saturday, he would share the Good News of Jesus with the black people of the community at the blacksmith shop, the grist mill, and the village store.

All the while, he spent extra hours teaching Rosa the Bible and the Lutheran Confessions for her teaching and missionary work.

On Palm Sunday, just four months after he first stepped foot off the train, Rev. Bakke baptized 58 women, men, and children and confirmed another 70. The first head he laid his hand upon was Rosa's, making her the first black Lutheran confirmed in Alabama.

Rosa became the first black Lutheran confirmed in Alabama.

On Easter Sunday, Christ Lutheran in Rosebud was formally organized as the mother church in rural Alabama, along with its school. By the end of 1916, there were 187 baptized and 122 confirmed members.

From the one school, begun by a faith-filled servant of the Lord, more than 35 congregations and preaching stations were founded over the next decades, with a total membership of 3,212. There were 30 Lutheran schools serving 1,227 children.

True to her calling, Rosa went wherever she was needed, starting schools, teaching religion and academics, and once even paying for workers to dig a well so her schoolchildren would have water.

It was the Living Water that filled her heart with the deepest joy and took her around the country, raising funds from Lutheran churches and missionary societies to better serve her people.

How many memories came flooding back to her from that simple scene.

◆ ◆ ◆
chapter five
A Dream Realized

Rosa looked out at the field of cotton growing next to the campus of the Alabama Lutheran
Academy in Selma. It was a sea of white, ready to
harvest.

How many memories came flooding back
to her from that simple scene, as she recalled
Christ's call to share the Good News with His
people, "Lift up your eyes, and look on the fields;
for they are white already to harvest" (John 4:35b
KJV).

Her lifelong dream had been realized in
ways she could never imagine. At 52, she stood
on the campus of Alabama Lutheran Academy,
a high school and junior college to train teachers
for the many Lutheran schools she had helped
start. From its humble beginnings in a rented
Selma cottage in 1922, the campus now boasted
a chapel, dormitories, classrooms, and a library.

She had answered the call to the Academy
in 1946 and loved teaching religion to eighth
grade boys and girls, who she fervently prayed
would become pastors and teachers for her

beloved Lutheran Church. And as her younger brothers and sisters could attest, she expected Bible memory work to be mastered!

She had prayed all her life to live God's will and to serve her people. She thanked God for granting her this heart's desire, even when she was too sick to stand. She thanked God for the beautiful people He had brought into her life beginning with her faith-filled parents, her brothers and sisters, then her extended family including great nieces and nephews, many of whom had become Lutheran teachers and pastors.

With deep thankfulness, she thought of the faithful women and men who had worked alongside the church, like Priscilla and Aquilla, who had helped Paul (Romans 16:3).

Twin sisters Mary and Sarah McCants were such good students, truly on fire for the Lord while they boarded with her at Rosebud. After their confirmation at Christ Church, the young women wanted to start a Lutheran Sunday School in their hometown of Vredenburgh.

Rosa smiled thinking of how hard those two young women worked, scrubbing out the old log cabin their father let them use for their school. She could still picture them hammering seats out of old pieces of a wagon body and carrying them to the school on top of their heads!

She thought of Mr. Alex Etheridge, an old man wearing filthy clothes who often stopped and sat under the oak tree in the schoolyard at Rosebud, listening through the window. "Let's send him off, he looks like a tramp," one of the teachers said. "No, I'll speak to him," Rosa replied.

She pictured them carrying the seats to the school on top of their heads!

"When I gets off work at the sawmill, I likes to come listen to your preacher," Mr. Etheridge had told her. "I feel too dirty to come in your nice church. But could you start a church near my home?"

After Mr. Etheridge had reached many in Possum Bend to build interest in a Lutheran Church, Our Savior Lutheran School and Church were founded that Thanksgiving, growing into the largest Lutheran School in the area.

Possum Bend Lutheran Church

She remembered Baptist Pastor Cornelius Smith, who wanted a Lutheran church and school to serve tenant farmers on Judge B. M. Miller's plantation in Midway, Alabama. We started that school at the request of a Baptist minister in a deserted Presbyterian school building, she thought. When her family lived in Hamburg, Rosa started a school there.

Sometimes her poor feet could still feel the hundreds of miles she had put on them, trodding through muddy washed-out roads and deep into fields, seeking souls for Jesus. She had always wanted to give a Christian education to her people, but until she met the Lutherans, she did not know what that meant.

As clear as a school bell, her people heard the saving Gospel from Lutheran teachers and pastors who brought Christ's light to the "Black Belt" of Alabama. *For it is by grace you have been saved through faith* (Ephesians 2:8).

Faith shone brightly in the face of dear "Aunt" Fannie Steele. Rosa remembered her sitting in her homemade rocker near the flickering warmth of her small fire in the little hut out in the pine hills.

"I can't read, but I can tell the good story of our Savior!" Aunty told Rosa.

Born into slavery, Aunt Fannie had spent backbreaking years picking cotton for her owners and losing family to the auction block. She never learned to read and owned little.

But Aunt Fannie was filled with joy because one night she heard the Gospel preached at a Lutheran meeting in a nearby log cabin.

"I can't read, but I can tell the good story of our Savior!" Aunty told Rosa. She was such an evangelist that she helped found two more Lutheran churches nearby. "Thank you, Miss Rosa," she said, tears streaming down her wrinkled deep brown face. "Now I really know what it feels like to be free. Thank God I'm free at last!"

Yes, looking out on the cotton fields brought Rosa's life full circle. She could still hear sainted Pastor Bakke as he confirmed her into her life's ministry so many years ago. Placing his worn hand on her head, he recited her Bible verse, which had carried her through years of faithfulness to the Lord and to the church:

> *Be confident of this, that He who began a good work in you will carry it on to completion until the day of Christ Jesus.*
> Philippians 1:6 NIV

Portrait of Rosa J. Young

hero of
faith

✦ ✦ ✦
Epilogue:

Rosa Jinsey Young was awarded an honorary doctorate from Concordia Seminary, St. Louis, in 1961 for her years of dedicated service, the first woman to receive the honor. She died June 30, 1971, after a lengthy illness and is buried at her beloved home church in Rosebud, Alabama. Her tombstone states:

Pioneer Missionary . . .
Who Initiated Lutheran Christian Education
among black people in Alabama.

Timeline of Events

during Rosa Young's Life

1890 Rosa J. Young is born in Rosebud, AL, on May 14 to Grant and Nancy Young

1896 U.S. Supreme Court legalizes segregation in *Plessy vs. Ferguson*

1900 Rosa is baptized into the African Methodist Church at age 10

1901 Booker T. Washington publishes his autobiography *Up from Slavery*

1903 The Wright Brothers make their first flight

1903 Rosa leaves for Payne University to begin high school

1909 Rosa graduates as valedictorian from Payne University on June 1

1909– 1912 Rosa teaches at many different schools in Alabama

1912 Rosa opens a school in her hometown of Rosebud, AL

1914   World War I begins

1914   Cotton-destroying Mexican boll weevils
reach Alabama

1915   Rosa tries, unsuccessfully, to sell her
school to the African Methodist Episcopal
Church

1915   Rosa writes Booker T. Washington for
financial help for her school

1915   Rosa writes Pastor Drewes of The
Lutheran Church—Missouri Synod

1915   Rev. Nils J. Bakke arrives to see Rosa and
her school on December 17

1916   LCMS Mission Board decides to officially
enter Alabama; Rev. Bakke returns to
Rosebud to begin mission work

1916   Rev. Bakke baptizes 58 and confirms
70 on Palm Sunday

1918   World War I ends

1920   Nineteenth Amendment is passed,
giving women the right to vote

1922 Rosa helps found the Alabama Lutheran Academy in Selma, AL

1927 Miss Viola Wehrs writes to Rosa, asking for a description of her life before becoming a Lutheran; the resulting letter served as the foundation for Rosa's autobiography

1929 Stock market crash marks the beginning of the Great Depression

1930 Rosa publishes her autobiography, *Light in the Dark Belt: The Story of Rosa Young as Told by Herself*, with Concordia Publishing House

1939– World War II
1945

1946– Rosa teaches at the Alabama Lutheran
1961 Academy

1950 *Light in the Dark Belt* is reprinted in a paperback edition

1954 U.S. Supreme Court overturns the 1896 ruling, making segregation illegal in *Brown vs. Board of Education*

1955 Bus boycott begins when Rosa Parks refuses to give up her seat

1961 Rosa Young is awarded an honorary doctorate from Concordia Seminary for her dedicated service

1964 Martin Luther King Jr. receives the Nobel Peace Prize

1971 Rosa Young dies at age 81 on June 30

◆ ◆ ◆
Acknowledgments

As a life-long Lutheran, I had never heard of Rosa Young. Then my husband and I moved to Mississippi and joined a Lutheran congregation led by Rev. Mark Griffin, whose father was from rural Alabama and had been a Rosa Young student.

Of course we joined them in attending our first Rosebud celebration in Wilcox County, Alabama, finding Christ Lutheran Church down a barely even dirt road off a two-lane highway. During the children's talk, we heard about Rosa Young and her ministry to the black poor in the early 1900s. I was astonished and inspired and hoped one day to write about her—thank you CPH!

I couldn't have put together these pages without the invaluable help of the men and women who knew her. My thanks goes to:

Mary Jones Wise and her family,
great-nieces and nephews of Dr. Young, who grew up not far from their great-aunt's home and shared personal recollections of the hard-working, dedicated teacher as well as family stories about the Youngs, including slave accounts of her parents.

Rev. James Wiggins Sr.,

who 'introduced' me to Rosa Young as the organizer of the annual Rosebud Festival. Now retired, Rev. Wiggins studied under Dr. Young at Alabama Lutheran Academy and led many of the rural congregations she began.

Rev. John Davis

of St. Paul Lutheran Church in Oak Hill, whose first teacher was Rosa Young at a tiny two-room shed in Catherine, Alabama. Dr. Young was also his first Vacation Bible School teacher. Rev. Davis has a long history of service in Lutheran churches of Alabama, and a collection of photos and articles of the early mission years.

Rev. McNair Ramsey,

pastor of Immanuel Lutheran church in Vredenburgh and former acting president at Concordia College, who gave me access to the Rosa Young Museum on the college campus.

Rev. Thomas Nunes,

retired pastor of St. Paul Lutheran in Birmingham and historian of Lutherans in Alabama, who provided many valuable articles about the early years of the church in this state.

David and Joe Ellwanger,

whose father, Rev. Walter, headed up the Lutheran ministry in rural Alabama from 1945 to 1967. They shared some boyhood recollections of Dr. Young, who stayed briefly after an illness at their home in Selma (which is my home now).

Dr. Rosa Young,

whose autographed copy of her book *Light in the Dark Belt* appeared on a sale shelf at Concordia, River Forest library for 25 cents when I was a graduate student there. It is truly astonishing what she accomplished in the poverty of rural Alabama during days of deep discrimination. She truly fixed her eyes on Jesus! (Hebrews 12:2 NIV)

I pray Rosa Young's inspiring story of great faith and fearless determination leads many young men and women into Lutheran ministry— that would be her greatest joy.

Christine S. Weerts
Selma, Alabama